Looking . . . Seeing

Looking... Seeing

poems and song lyrics by Harry Chapin

with drawings by Rob White

Thomas Y. Crowell Company
Established 1834   New York

ISBN: 0-690-01657-3

LIBRARY OF CONGRESS CATALOG CARD NUMBER: 77-11564

78 79 80 81 82 10 9 8 7 6 5 4 3 2 1

This book was edited by and is dedicated to
Sandy Chapin,
a better poet than I will ever be.

contents

poems

song lyrics

Autobiographical Notes

poems

1. *rising tide*

The afternoon sun
moves across the floor.
It heads towards my feet,
out to catch me.

My window spills it through.
It splashes off the floor
and makes fiery drops
of the airborne dust in my writing room.

Now it touches my shoe
and starts up my leg.
It rises like the water's mark
up the pilings of a dock.

The light arrives to wash
the cluttered table top.
It soaks the open books
and floats my pencils and pens.

It turns my ink-filled pages
into shimmering reflectors
sending senseless lightspots
into the corners of the walls.

The liquid I've been writing on
is mirrored by the door.
Before the light can reach my eyes
I leap to get my coat, chased out
to swim or loudly drown.

2. *changing of the guard*

The old poet starts
the heavy trek to the podium.
The slow bulk of his greatcoat
brings the illusion
of a great weight moving.

His hair is struck translucent
by the noonday sun.
The strands have passed beyond the white
and are reapproaching yellow.

The farmer's hand that clasps
the windwhipped pages
is flecked with the specks
that mark old wood.

He stands waiting as silence
assembles across the crowded Avenue.
The wind sputters on the microphones.

His voice starts vaguely,
an old saw seaching for the groove.
Words hunched out at a farm
melt in the Washington day.

A tophat is offered to cast
its black silk shadow.
Behind it he retrieves
the sinew of his lines.

He speaks of harvests
and of lifelong sowing
of sweat into rocky soil.
Then the old poet is done.

Applause eases him to a seat
as already another voice
is flinging youth against the sun.

But one who has seen so many springs
does not regret winter's coming.
A life progressed so competently
up to its end stands
ready to encompass death.

3. *the royal kingdom*

She sat the stoop like an emerald throne,
a three year old queen
with serfslop hands to prop her chin.
Some daredevil or court jester
could have made a sporting quip
about the less than courtly knees
that had heedlessly emerged
from her tattered cotton dress.
But her wide brown eyes
dreamed true regality.

And seeing her
that adult afternoon
I for the first time
in my own few years
felt envy of the youth
that let life lie
deliciously complete,
and made her the ruler of
The Land of Anticipation.

4. *the great divide*

INTERSTATE 80 IS OPEN FOR TRAFFIC
The sign says so and I've stopped
beside the entrance ramp, wondering
If I get on
can I get off?

One hundred yards ahead
there's six wide lanes
speeding off to somewhere.
It's twilight
or does that sky say dawn?

The sullen light shows clean concrete.
The landscaped grass is coming slow if at all.
There are no oil stains,
no skid marks, accidents or billboards.
At most a waysign or two.
Is someone waiting?

Standing beside the car
the wind tugs at my trousers
with doubts about my path.
Shall I turn home?

Old familiar Route 46
slides back down behind me.
A vast junkyard of accordion cars,
decapitated dolls, sodden books,
the glitter of shattered bottles.
But the McDonald stands still thrive
selling gas and everything but dreams.
A gust kicks up a rusting can.
In the distance there's thunder
or is it crumbling walls?

I stand at the Great Divide.
Thirty years gone, no longer trusted.
The highway ahead is as empty
as the old road behind.
Is anything sure these days?

I cram myself back in,
check gauges and turn the key.
Gun it, Kid.
Hit the ramp
with horsepower going for you.
Cradled in my Detroit casket,
transistors beating my eardrums,
of course I'm going on.
This senseless push the only claim
I have on some divinity.

5. *the summer of '64*

Now of course
he was back at school,
but the fuzzy faced Brooklyn kid
with the ban-the-bomb pin
and the we-shall-overcome guitar
had spent the summer in Mississippi.
He'd befriended black boys
older than his father,
eaten grits and collard greens,
sat with black girls
at bloody counters
and walked a thousand miles.
He'd rebuilt blasted churches
while the sweat streamed in rivulets
down his pimple blemished back,
and faced the loutish drawling
of the troopers from the state
with his peach of a chin held high.

after English class
and his books at night,
he slept and had a wetdream
about anygirl, the one
he'd never had.

6. *an admission*

Being modern
and agnosticated
I don't possess a God
to push and pull about
to match fate's idle motions.

But every once in a while,
not very often
let me add quickly,
being only human
I am prone to feeling
lost and somewhat minuscule.
Shyly I place
some sort of Being,
entirely nonreligious
let me assure you,
above me in the firmament.

I let Him laugh
at my endeavors
and grant myself,
only at these weakened moments,
the grace of Someone
Else's recognition
of my very doubtful
existence.

7. the rain bridge

It was going to rain,
that first day in the country.
I felt the waiting in the air
as we went to fill the buckets
at the pump before the storm.
My grandfather's rocking tread
led the way as I bounced after,
new dungarees crisp on my legs,
sneakers unscuffed and white,
a pail swinging from each fist.

The farm always marked
the last weeks of my vacation.
I hadn't seen him since last summer
or really known him ever.
He was country strange,
living a self imposed exile
to give perspective to the world.
The critics said his books
showed the difference—
"clearheaded observations,
difficultly related."

The board covered well
was tree sheltered, standing
beside the rock-walled field
that leaned towards the lake.
He bent and hooked a bucket
over the spout and grunted—
"It will be coming soon."

The lake and land were truly his.
He'd built the dam and cleared
the fields, forty years worth.
The sweating simplicity took
writer's worries off his mind.
And here he reigned a shy patriarch,
his children and their broods
welcomed but subtle tenants.

I took my stance,
the cast iron cold in my palms.
I rammed the handle down.
The gasping of the leather washers
cut through the still air
and seemed to start the wind.
I pumped harder and well water
choked up and splashed cleanly
in the bottom of the five gallon pail.

One of the early-dried late summer leaves,
loosed into the wind by swaying trees,
searched out the filling bucket.
Grandfather leaned and dipped it out,
scolding as I slowed—"Hurry up, boy.
It'll reach the lake in a minute."

The trees now tossed in earnest,
dancing excitement above my head.
The sucking of the plunger
added its raucous call as I hurried
trying to fill the last of the buckets.
My grandfather called over the noise,
an unexpected shaking in his voice—
"It's gonna be a heller!"

I pushed the water up to the line
in the pail and turned to see
the wall of rain come across the lake.
I felt like yelling something
and then he shouted suddenly—
"Come on, rain you Big Bastard!
Rain!"

And it was coming,
bending down the long grass
as it swept across the field.
I started howling something
into the impossible loudness.

When the rain hit,
he was shaking his fist at the sky,
both of us still shouting.
The noise steadied to
the constant drumming of striking

He turned sheepishly.
I looked back at him and grinned.
Soaked, we picked up the buckets
and walked unhurriedly back
through the rain.

8. *chauvinist prayer*

A model of a thoroughbred,
slim and leggy, sleekly groomed,
strides the perfect gait
to equate 5th Avenue with Churchill Downs.

We dreamers and connoisseurs
nod and note her flawless form,
check off the expert's list:
Hocks—slim, rump—firm, good flanks.

Full chest, high head, glistening mane.
This one's built for speed.
You couldn't help but hope
to add her to your stable.

But she goes to garner roses.
You wouldn't want to waste
that restless shape and harness her
to plod behind a plow and break her.

She gains the spotlit circle
from where she shows her special graces
by wearing blinders when she races.
No time to stop and graze beyond the fence.

We say among us as she bursts on past
us sluggish nine-to-fiver plugs
that we will last a longer pull
while rambling at our slower paces.

But still,
to ride her,
just once,
in the Derby!

9. *a double edged rib*

He said:
    "Baby, can I do it, can I do it?"
    And as she let him
    she couldn't help but worry
    as it had never been used before
    if that was all he wanted.

    After he had done it
    it never fit the same again.

She said:
    "Honey, I want it, I want it?"
    And as he gave it to her
    he couldn't help but wonder
    if he would ever get it back.

    Later she returned it,
    but it was bent.

10. *baptismal*

I used to think
that girls never went
to the bathroom,
and that by some
incredibly intricate
phenomena
no waste came
from their magically
forbidden orifices.

Then at sixteen,
my first love,
a seventeen year old
gum chewing angel,
with deadly accuracy,
shat on me.

11. *plains crossing*

Only the poles rear
to pierce the horizon.
The tableland is flat,
stretched out to the sky's brim.
There the grey starts upwards,
folds over and meets
the dark plains behind.

The tarred row of tall black crosses
connects the flat and grey.
I'm restless in the pattern
of this endless skinny cemetery.
I search for deviations—
a pole shifted by long forgotten frosts,
a stretch of line,
loose and slack from an ice storm.

I bounce my eyes
from windshield to rearview mirror,
watching the poles wax and wane.
Ahead they loom like oracles,
then the mirror sucks
them into a tiny hole.

Without thinking
I thread the miles with the lines,
string them through the poles
and leave them beside the road.

The poles,
the lines,
the miles,
the time,
sagging, sagging
until...

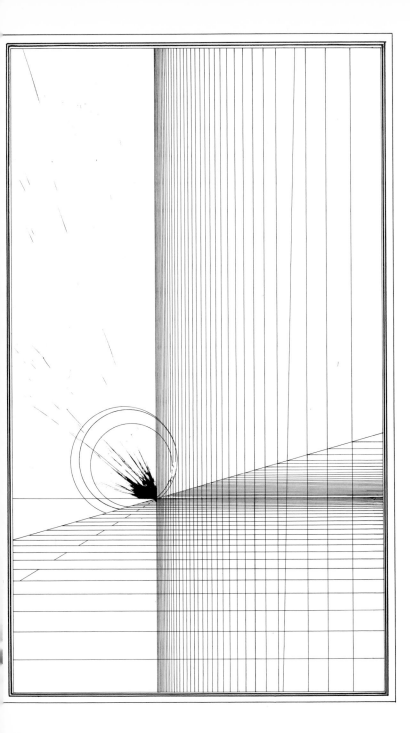

the taut shriek
of rubber on the road,
the shattered windshield
and blood.

12. *somersault for my daughter*

When I was a child
I had to climb a tree.
Tallness got to me.
The years went by with higher trees
and me on hills and mountain peaks.
Where I couldn't reach
I used the wings that man
has made for scaling things.
The sun and stars I couldn't climb
I stretched and scaled in my mind
and seldom worried at what's left behind.

A time came when heights were dark
and tallness less and not a more.
I never felt so lost before.
She came from somewhere
and simply said—"Daddy,
go stand on your head!"

I did, all foolish pride long gone.
Turned around, head to the ground,
upside down yet suddenly rightside up.
There was the ceiling, the top,
the end for fancy's wildest flyer
comfortable inches from my head.
Try as I might there was no higher,
I had to look around instead.

I saw a dangling tree,
no heaven pointed spire,
with roots digging in to hold the ground.
And mountains climbing not up but down
The stars, shiny pebbles
for my feet to play around.

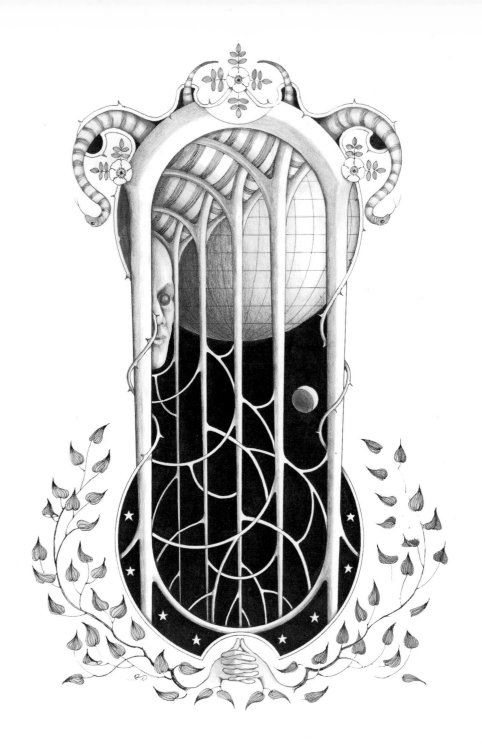

13. *butterflies*

One eye,
lizardlike,
opens on my pillow.
My dreams demand
some sustenance
from this encroaching day.

I close again
for one last view
of where I've been.
My hackles rise in terror
at images of razor claws.
I sharpen my fangs.

My alarm clock's timid fanfare
draws me to its blunted blades
tracing placid circles.
My feet find the floor.
I gird myself with cotton,
strap on ballpoint swords

swagger forth
to search the streets
for concrete lists
reverberating with chimes
of metal and savage duels.
But all the lions are gone.

I stride into arenas,
legs spread, eyes ready
to be slaked by rosy rivulets.
But there are no torn
and blood-enobled dead,
made victors with their vanquishing.

There is only muffled swishing.
Park benches hold casualties of silent wars,
each one found too proud or weak
to swing against a fluttering mark.
No chance for decent burial.
They lug their own sarcophagi.

Still I, a virgin warrior
who dreams of bright medallions,
must battle with the butterflies,
or else be bleached and broken
by pale and stealthy
powdered wings.

14. *peace teachers*

The woman smacked her whining kid
and he shrieked all the louder.
Then he looked out through dry eyes
and scratched her leg again.
Her husband was shaking him
as I passed by.

On TV that evening
I saw all three of them
picketing the White House
carrying a sign saying—
FAMILIES
AGAINST WAR
AS AN INSTRUMENT
OF NATIONAL POLICY.

15. *double image*

Mornings I search for my whiplash
wastrel in the looking glass,
opting for far more magical fare
than the tangible bulk
of that burgher there.
Still mourning the death
of the Cowboy Kid
I coax the mirror
to return my bully boy,
vaguely sweet and dim defined.

But today, before showering,
I cringe at the forecast:
time's thickening collar
circles my waist, signaling
the day when touching my toe
will be forcing a rusty hinge.
And I try to look through
this window to a place
I no longer own.

16. *counterpoint*

Thick soles crush
    the damp grass.
A dark column moves in to mar
    the bright face of summer.
    A squirrel runs for cover.
The black robed bride
brings her blind shadow
    to the bustle of the meadow.
    Grasshoppers, in doubt
    halt their clicks and scrapes.
Blunt toes push upwards
    towards a grassy rise.
    Birds roost to eye
    the passing shape.
She stops atop the knoll
and each of twenty centuries
of righteous fire and water
bends her frail and fervent back.
    The wind hangs in the trees.
She stills the smart of pain
    from the twisted twig beneath her knee
and lifts her parchment face
    above the sun drenched hollows,
    above the languid trees
    and silent sparrows,
    above the secular summer sky.
    But the sun's impartial stare
burns her dark accustomed eyes.
She plants a tightlaced shoe to rise.
She dwindles with her homeward tread.
    The glen resumes its ragtag choir.
Returning to her cloistered bed
the widow leaves intact
    the meadow's maidenhead.

17. revelry

Walking on an autumn hill
the windblown wine has turned my head.
I fling my arms and scatter leaves,
churning fire and crimson
behind my drunken heels.

The chipmunks rattle with me too,
but with business on their minds.
They scold my tippler's aimlessness
and chatter in their hurry
to scavenge winter fodder.

The clouds have shredded into musty puffs,
feathers skim the horizon.
Flocks of toiling wings and feathers
blow south—cawing, honking, receding.

And I, the solitary celebrant
at summer's wake,
call and curse above the din.
I have learned what the Irish know,
coarse shouts trap tears
behind the silver screen of revelry.

18. *one simple question*

Why,
I said to myself,
with one and a half billion
women in the world,
more or less,
must I lie here
and play night's
silly fluted tune
unaccompanied?

Especially
as I am sure
that a goodly portion
of that one and a half billion
are unaccompanied
and humming
the same
quick fingered
melody.

19. *spectator sport*

He was drunk with love,
the love he thought
he was in, flying high
and slightly silly.

She watched him, curious.

She saw him spew days forth,
frothy glee in each augmented taste.
And clutch nights close
singing slightly off key
at the brighter moon and stars.
He even wove some dandelions
for her golden crown.

But just about then
she walked away
wondering—
"Why all the fuss?"

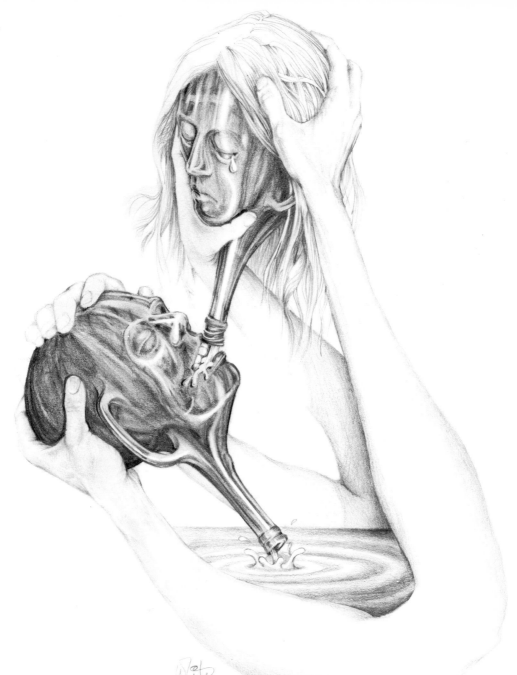

20. *consummation*

She looked clumsy
as her skirt crumpled.
He shifted feet beside the bed.

They had passed the preliminaries
during countless backseat nights
of inches and recriminations.

A lock of hair swung
to mercifully close the door
ajar there in her eyes.

He glanced at her thighs
where the tan stopped
and the staring tuft waited.

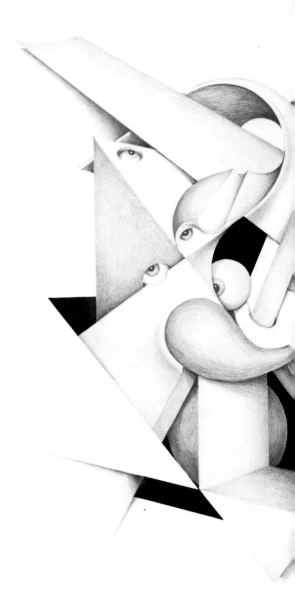

Afterward
she was wet in his arms
and he comforted her shoulder.

The TV set didn't blink.
The motel room
was noncommittal.

They, at least,
had gone through this
a thousand times before.

21. *the quiet answer*

I often wondered how
the abundance of the sky
was stroked by luminous fingers
from a far off celestial ball,

and how the small moon
gathered all the scattered dark
and shed it off its own pale curve
to mold the night's immense asymmetry,

and how the call of a solitary bird
could shred the deepest forest silence
making subsequent silence
more eloquent than the song itself,

until you brought the quiet answer
when your second smile rephrased infinity.

22. *seascape*

You are the nighttime sea, immense
and deep, in eternal variance.
The moonmad sky, entranced, descends
in its romance to kiss your skin

and dance your hollows and billowing swells.
Above the whisper as waves embrace
the night wind breathes a seawise sigh—
"Beware of dangers that lurk below."

Yes, your undersea currents tell
of salt exploding on blackened shoals,
the rage of a murderous surf
waiting to crush the stoutest craft.

But I sail on as the sailor must sail,
keeping the watch that the sailor must keep,
risking the teeth of your dark hung shores
for the rapturous rhythms that rise from the deep.

23. *pandora's box*

The brown crocodile eyes,
lazy and deep lidded
were drifting downward
to reptilian depths.

It was her night look,
and didn't fit her Scarsdale days.
With those blue-nosed lights
her body froze into the warm
resiliency of a pair of pliers.

But now alone, save one,
with Old Faithful's steaming geyser
seeking her chameleon thighs,
she played deliberately with her hair
and swung the magic portal wide.

The fine boned patrician
invites my common pleasure,
deliciously aware of impending sins.

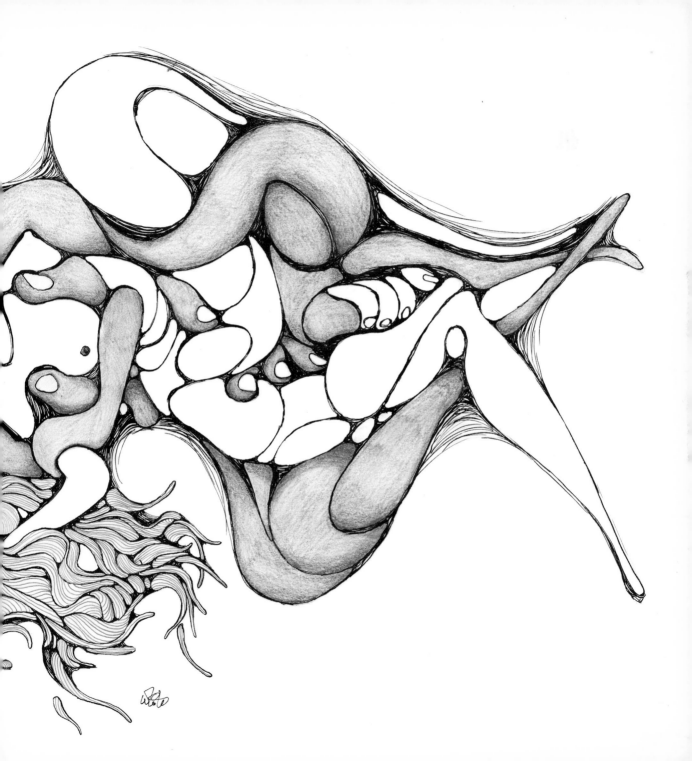

24. *skirmish*

The rank taste of bile
burns my mouth
and I, pridethick
let our backs diverge,
a dueler uncertain
when to turn and fire.

The night, benign and unmaligned,
squats smug with its new moon
brighter than a streetlight.
A ventriloquist with your voice
down pat festers inside.

"Fool" your proxy snarls.
"Bitch" I volley back.
My heels are machine guns
covering my retreat.

The house looms large.
I search the rooms
for some truce banner.
They too have been bloodied
by this uncivil war,
fought with one who strikes too well.
Long practice grooves the aim.

Who-I-left-you-left-me?
I struggle with self pity,
a soldier naked
on a cold dark field.

What can I do
but wash in sullen tears
and somehow try to gather
the tattered blanket of sleep.

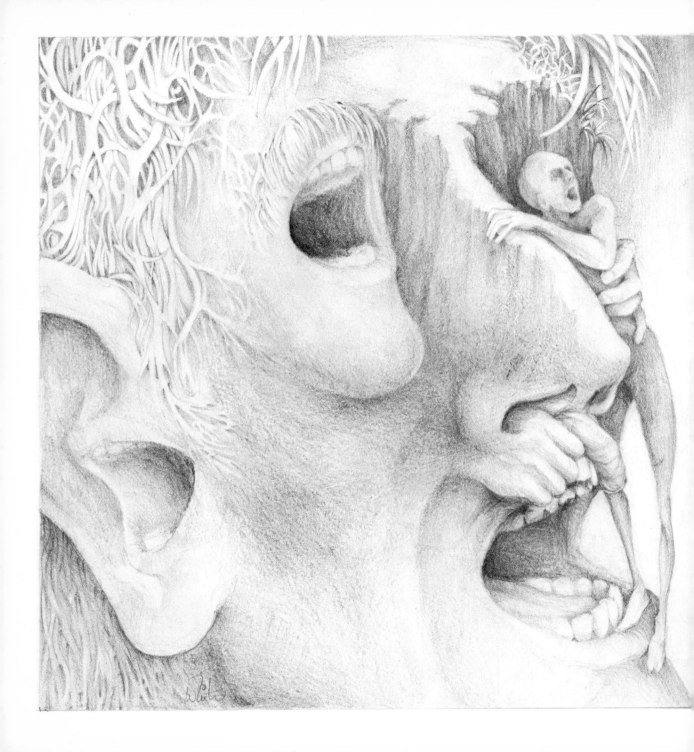

25. *curses*

Damn this soft drawn night
    with its blatant lovers sky
    and obvious breeze, rustling through
    my faceless neighbor's maple trees.

Damn this stupid dark that brings
    me back so late from flicker picture shows
    where old men wheeze and slump in their seats
    and rape the rationale of my cheap escapes.

Damn the clock that clicks,
    nasal motors, muttering cars
    that scurry through the murky spots
    to pause at corner pools of light.

Damn this itch of wrinkled sheets,
    the confines of this bed
    too wide to sleep alone
    and too small to hide inside.

Damn the dreadful baldness
    of each self-pitying whine
    that simmers unreleased,
    not rating tears.

Damn this state that drives me to discover
    that curses screamed at loneliness
    call only the scant comfort
    of all mankind's answering echo.

26. *collision*

The sun
    threading
    through the

                    Spring-fresh
            leaves

                            makes a
                                dappled
                                shifting
                                    pattern

                                            on the sidewalk

until it rams into
the hulking bulk
of the warehouse.

27. departure

They brought us in from play
to touch her when she died
so as not to fear from death

and we were afraid.

Her daughters busied all around,
cackling over the silent bed.
They'd done the same before she died,
she'd been long gone to them,

not us.

Slowfooting through our croquet games
she cheered us as we played,
taught us cards on rainy days
and when the weather cleared

watched us

whoop and bang
between the rocks and trees.
When we fell and bruised or bled
she gave her lap to cry—

"No matter."

Quietly she ate
except when sipping soup.
Our parents talked above her,
her daughters and their daughters—
"She doesn't know." "Her hearing's gone."
She'd move her head,
pale eyes would close
to look beyond the window.

We looked at our plates.

One breakfast time she did not come
carefully down the backroom stairs.
Swiftly we were sent to play.
We saw the doctor come and go,

too quickly.

Then we were called
and walked beside the silent bed.
We stood and had our hands brought forth
to touch that eyeless face.

We knew she wasn't there.

We didn't play that day.

From our beds we heard them talk,
parceling out her memories.

28. *a child at night on a country road*

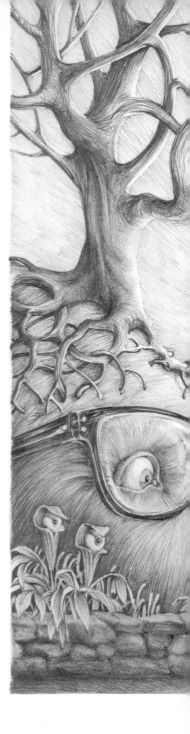

A child at night
on a country road.
It is dark
and he is alone.
The stars blink
so far above
surely they're not meant
to come along.
The moon is down.
It shines out round
one night in four.

A child at night
on a lonely road.
A well lit place
so far ahead it's lost
behind the trees
that line the way.
There's no light
and ears exceed their duty.
Small things rustling
in the shadows expand
into metaphors for fear.

A child at night
on an empty road.
If he fears to follow on,
if he hears his footsteps
cease, if he lets the midnight
wind catch him where
he stands, it's over.
So he goes on.
A child at night
on a country road.

29. *service*

The two of them stood
at Sunday morning's door
hoping that Jehovah
was witnessing their mission.
The skinny small town boy
and the cowbreasted farmless girl
who asked in an earnest bedroom voice
"Have you ever thought about the Resurrection?"

The world came smashing back on my shoulders.

All I could do was stand
sleepy headed in my shorts
and wish for all of us
that I had.

30. *missed connection*

The girl on the subway
was THE ONE. I knew
there could never be
another like her.

She looked down at her hands,
squeezed the Hunter College notebook
and looked up again
through her lashes.

I told myself that
if I didn't have this bulky suitcase
and awkward guitar I would follow her,
and then I got off at my stop.

She looked at me
through the dirty window
as the cars jerked
and pulled away.

31. *transition*

My memory of our fulcrum day
is caught between the cool befores
and molten afters.
My mind resists your flowered print,
prim and Kodak pretty,
the last attempt at crisp preemption
of our melting senses.
But neither do I focus on
that steamswept view of you
I knew as curling spans of nudity
fused us both together.

My memory of that day
is trapped in our transition—
you, thrust from the car,
toes seeking the curb,
one knee too widely swinging.
A streetlight's artless flash
records a daring gleam of thigh
and you, hand and eye both raised,
awash in sudden wonder,
aware of our undoing.

32. *convergence*

Outside the moon had curled
pared down to a sliver.
As if full from that feast
each star hung gorged and glistening.

Gaunt restless puffs raced the wind
across the midnight silver
and teased the landlocked trees
to break their fetters.

The falling leaves, fresh gilded
for their first and final flight,
chatter as they rouse the shutters
to swing and clatter.

Your knee warmbending on my thigh
we fall through summer's ending,
still fresh from flinging
savage colors at the night.

33. *irrigation*

When the lemon sun
has squeezed the day too dry,
then I am most glad of you.
All your moist mouths pour forth
sweet springs to replenish me.
You, with your softly damp designs
are like a gentle engineer,
shoring up the breaches in the dike,
storing cool midnight rain against a drought.
When the day has curled up dry,
I sleep immersed in you.

And as tomorrow yawns
out its first hot breath
I can go out, freshly green,
with your yellow morning dandelion
implanted in the buttonhole of me.

34. *dissonance*

The raucous sun is an affront
spitting forth fires
that should have been doused
by the pools in my eyes.

The wind struts
through the trees.
Each in turn takes up
his neighbor's drunken dance.

The children wail like banshees
in the grassy fields of Central Park.
The kerchiefed mothers
sew and scandal in the shade.

But back in our room
your empty closet sits—
a gutted chapel
robbed of its crucifix.

35. *calling card*

My nose,
an eager beagle
not by choice,

often leads off on a howling chase,
lured by the crimson herring
of your familiar fragrance.

My mind is bounced along,
straining on the leash that tries
to collar prideless senses.

Your perfume is too popular.
Today it was a bulky blonde,
bleached past all belief.

I wish that you had picked
a far less common scent
to be your representative.

But still it serves you well
and brings you back most tangibly
with every strap and hair intact—

that dab between your lace cupped breasts.
The coup staged by my senses
is thwarted temporarily,

still sniffing for another trace,
whining for their fickle queen,
restless in a shaky peace.

36. *daily news*

At eight o'clock each evening
he comes for the news.
He huddles by the fence
at the subway exit's stand,
out of the wind,
out of the winter
that knows no approaching spring.

Soon the truck rumbles up.
The smack of bundles on pavement
jolts him, he turns his head
to watch the careless jumble.
Undershirted men haul and stack
the piles and maul the comic strips.

He stoops to pick below
for untorn print. He fingers
through his change. News
cradled in his arms, he inches
back to uneventful rooms
to glean his day from
folded picture pages bound with wire.

37. *postscript*

Poets seem
to dwell on death
and mouth its meaning
endlessly.

Until,

a trifle bored,
it flicks its noiseless finger
and stills the chatter
deadly.

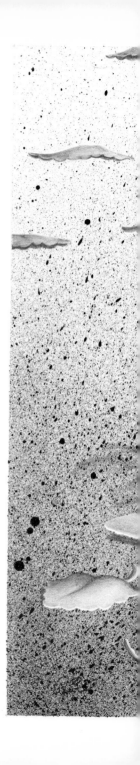

38. self portrait

The stacks of my factory
prod the night
making it howl
like a mistreated cur.
Flames lap the dark,
gluttons for air,
slobbering out soot
on my barbaric spree.
The ravenous light
spreads the riotous scene—
my mongrel's desecration
of the Lord's High Hall.
I sprawl and guzzle
and maul the landscape
with rabid industry.

But a shy pup's tears
sizzle on the charred bricks
of a smoldering kiln
in the dungeons deep below.

39. *droplets*

I am loath to
rest with silence.
It gathers
in my ears,
telling things
that should be done
and spouting out
best hidden doubts.

Rain is a busy peaceful noise.
Tracking brittle cross the roof.
Stepping
soft
from leaf
to leaf.
Working
drops
down
window panes.
Doing endless tiny things,
Precluding all but peace of mind.

40. *the shortest story*

I am born today
The sun burns its promise in my eyes
Mama strikes me and I draw a breath to cry
Far above a cloud softly tumbles through the sky
I am glad to be alive

It is my seventh day
I taste the hunger and I cry
Brother and sister cling to Mama's side
She squeezes her breast but it has nothing to provide
Someone weeps
I fall asleep

It is twenty days today
Mama does not hold me anymore
I open my mouth but I am to weak to cry
Far above a bird slowly crawls across the sky
Why is there nothing left to do but die?

song lyrics

41. *taxi*

It was raining hard in Frisco,
I needed one more fare to make my night,
A lady up ahead waved to flag me down,
She got in at the light.

"Where you going to my Lady Blue,
It's a shame you ruined your gown in the rain."
She just looked out the window,
She said, "16 Parkside Lane."

Something about her was familiar,
I could swear I seen her face before,
But she said, "I'm sure you're mistaken."
And she didn't say anything more.

It took a while but she looked in the mirror,
Then she glanced at the license for my name.
A smile seemed to come to her slowly.
It was a sad smile just the same.

And she said, "How are you, Harry?"
I said, "How are you, Sue?...
Through the too many miles and the too little smiles
I still remember you."

It was somewhere in a fairy tale,
I used to take her home in my car.
We learned about love in the back of a Dodge,
The lesson hadn't gone too far.

You see...
She was gonna be an actress,
And I was gonna learn to fly.
She took off to find the footlights,
I took off to find the sky.

I got something inside me,
To drive a princess blind.
There's a wild man wizard, he's hiding in me,
Illuminating my mind.
I got something inside me
Not what my life's about,
'Cause I been letting my outside tide me
Over 'til my time runs out.

CAUTION
DANGEROUS
INTERSECTION

Baby's so high that she's skying,
Yeah, she's flying, afraid to fall,
And I'll tell you why Baby's crying,
'Cause she's dying, aren't we all?

There was not much more for us to talk about,
Whatever we had once was gone.
So I turned the cab into the driveway,
Past the gate and the fine trimmed lawns.

And she said, "We must get together."
But I knew it'd never be arranged.
And she handed me twenty dollars for a two-fifty fare,
She said, "Harry, keep the change."

Well, another man might have been angry,
And another man might have been hurt,
But another man never would have let her go,
 stashed the bill in my shirt.

And she walked away in silence,
It's strange how you never know,
But we'd both gotten what we'd asked for,
Such a long, long time ago.

    You see . . .
    She was gonna be an actress,
    And I was gonna learn to fly.
    She took off to find the footlights,
    I took off for the sky.

And here she's acting happy,
Inside her handsome home,
And me, I'm flying in my taxi,
Taking tips and getting stoned.

 go flying so high when I'm stoned.

42. greyhound

It's midnight at the depot
and I drag my bags in line.
Traveling late, I got to go
but the bus won't be on time.
Everybody's looking half alive.
Later on the bus arrives.

They punch my ticket
I find a seat
and we move out past the lights.
Come on Driver, where's the heat?
It's cold out in the night.
I keep telling to myself that I don't care.
Come tomorrow, I'll be there.

Take the Greyhound.
It's a dog of a way to get around.
Take the Greyhound.
It's a dog gone easy way to get you down.

Tired of watching this night go by
so I look across the aisle.
The window's frosted, I can't sleep
but the girl returns my smile.
She reminds me of someone I knew back home.
So I doze. So it goes.

I'm wrinkled on my stool at the rest stop.
The waitress being cozy with the highway cop.
My coffee's tasting tired.
My eyes roll over dead.
Got to go outside and get the gas out of my head.
Oh, to be in bed.
You got me driving.
I'm on your Greyhound bus and you're driving.

But there's nothing new about Greyhounds.
Nothing new about feeling down.
Nothing new about putting off
or putting myself on.

Looking to tomorrow is the way the loser hides
I should have realized by now that all my life's a ride.
It's time to find some happy times and make myself some frien
I know there ain't no rainbows waiting when this journey ends

Stepping off this dirty bus first time I understood
It's got to be the going not the getting there that's good
That's a thought for keeping if I could.
It's got to be the going not the getting there that's good.

43. *bananas*

t was just after dark
when the truck started down
he hill that leads into Scranton Pennsylvania
   carrying thirty thousand pounds of bananas.

He was a young driver
ust out on his second job
and carrying the next day's pasty fruit
for everyone in that coal scarred city
where children play in backyard slagpiles
and people manage to eat each day
   about thirty thousand pounds of bananas.

He passed the sign that he should have seen
saying—Shift to low gear or fifty dollar fine, my friend.
He was thinking, perhaps
of the warm breathed woman
who was waiting at the journey's end.
He started down the two mile drop
the curving road that wound from the top of the hill,
pushing on through the shortening miles
that ran down to the depot, just a few more miles to go,
then he'd go home and have her ease
that long cramped day away and the smell
   of thirty thousand pounds of bananas.

He was picking up speed as the city spread
its twinkling lights below him.
But he paid no heed as a shivering thought
of the night's delights went through him.
His foot nursed the brakes to slow him down
but the pedal floored easy without a sound.
He said—Christ!
It was funny how he had named the only man
who could save him now.
He was trapped inside a dead end hellslide
for riding on his fear hunched back
was every one of those yellow green
   thirty thousand pounds of bananas.

He barely made the sweeping curve
that led into the steepest grade.
And he missed a thankful passing bus at ninety miles an hour.
He said—God, make it a dream
as he sideswiped nineteen neat parked cars,
clipped off thirteen telephone poles,
hit two houses, bruised eight trees
and Blue Crossed seven people.
It was then he lost his head
not to mention an arm or two, before he stopped.
And he smeared for four hundred yards
along the hill that leads into Scranton Pennsylvania
   all those thirty thousand pounds of bananas.

The toothless man who told me about it on the bus
as it went up the hill out of Scranton Pennsylvania
shrugged his shoulders, shook his head, and said—
   Man, it musta been somethin,
   Thirty thousand pounds of mashed bananas.

44. halfway to heaven

There's no tick tock on your electric clock
But still your life runs down

I'm halfway to heaven and my home in Forest Hills
It's halfpast eleven and I've got some time to kill
I missed my bus connection 'cause my train got in too late
And I'm forced into reflection by this half hour wait.

Now I have been a straight man and I've played it by the rules
I been a good man, a good husband, yes a good old fashioned fool.
I have a fine wife and two children just like everybody's got
But after fifteen years of marriage the fires don't burn too hot.

You see someone's played a trick on me.
They set me up so perfectly
Gave me their morality
And then changed the rules they set for me.
Someone must be laughing now,
Though it don't seem funny somehow,
How the world's accepting now
What they once would not allow
    Back in my younger days.
    The world has changed in so many ways.

My mother once said to me so many years ago now
Don't you touch those bad girls, so I never had girls
Until I had my Mary when we married
My Mary then had my two sons
My life as a lover it was already done
It was over before it had really begun

You see someone played a trick on me.
They sent this little girl to me,
She is my new secretary
And she's something to see.
    She's a nice girl, but it's a young world
    And she lives her life so free, and she sure gets thru to me

She brings her pad into my office, she wears a sweater and a skirt
And somewhere deep inside of me something starts to hurt.
She's wearing nothing underneath, and I can see what's there to see
And she smiles and says, "You wanted me?" and I'd have to agree.

You know how much I want her,
And I know that I could have her.
I know I could, I know she would
    Make love to me, so wonderfully.
    God Damn, I'm one horny mixed up mixture of a

In my head all my life I've been a sinner,
And in my bed with just my wife I'm still a beginner,
But tomorrow night I'm taking that little girl out to dinne

There's no tick tock on your electric clock
But still your life runs down.

45. *dogtown*

Up in Massachusetts there's a little spit of land
The men who make the maps, they call the place Cape Anne
The men who do the fishing call it Gloucester Harbor Sound
But the women left behind, they call the place Dogtown.

The men go out for whaling past the breakers and the fogs
The women stay home waiting, protected by the dogs.
A tough old whaler woman who had seen three husbands drown
Polled the population and she named the place Dogtown.

All those grey faced women in their black widows' gowns
Living in this graveyard granite town
You soon learn there's many more than one way to drown
That's when going to the dogs here in Dogtown.

My father was a merchant in the Boston fief
When my husband come and asked him for my hand
Little did I know then that a Gloucester whaler's wife
Marries but the sea salt and the sand.

He took me up to Dogtown the day I was a bride.
We had ten days together before he left my side.
He was the first mate of a whaling ship, the keeper of the log
He said: "Farewell my darling, I'm going to leave you with my dog."

I have seen the splintered timbers of a hundred shattered hulls
Known the silence of the granite and the screeching of the gulls
Heard that crazy Widow Cather walk the harbor as she raves
At the endless rolling whisper of the waves.

Sitting by the fireside, the embers slowly die
Is it a sign of weakness when a woman wants to cry?
The dog is closely watching, the fire glints in his eye.
No use to go to sleep this early no use to even try.

My blood beats like a woman's, I've got a woman's breasts and thighs
But where am I to offer them, to the ocean or the skies?

Living with this silent dog all these moments of my life
He's been my only husband. Am I a widow or his wife?

It's a Dog Town
And it's a fog town.
And there's nothing around 'cept the sea pounding granite ground.
And this black midnight horror of a hound.

Standing on this craggy cliff my eyes fixed on the sea
Six months past when his ship was due I'm a widow to be
For liking this half living with the lonely and the fog
You need the bastard of the mating of a woman and a dog.

I have seen the splintered timbers of a hundred shattered hulls
Known the silence of the granite and the screeching of the gulls
Heard that crazy Widow Cather walk the harbor as she raves
At the endless rolling whisper of the waves.

At the endless rolling whisper of the waves.

46. *womanchild*

Dripping streetlights, darkened buildings
Wandering head hung down low.
As she's walking she keeps wondering
Does her Mama know?
Where will she go?

Woman child your eyes are wild
The rain runs down your hair
Woman child, mercy mild
What will you tell your teddy bear?

He turned you on his solid body
electric Gibson guitar
His clever fingers searched and found
Exactly where you are.
You went too far.

It was an early morning phone call.
What news has been received.
A halting voice is telling him
What they have both conceived,
Asking how the dilemma can be relieved.

"I will give you the money, honey
And I'll set up a time.
But you got to go there on your own, Babe
Cause I don't know that it's mine."

Woman child.
Mama's little angel's been defiled.

She took a taxi to the clinic
Where they do the modern thing
A white-coat doctor laid her out
Said: You won't feel a thing
I got the sweet salvation that this
little ole knife can bring.
You don't have to worry 'bout no offspring.
That's that.
It's just a two hundred dollar mishap.
It don't mean a thing.
It's all over now
You can tell your singer to sing.

47. *pigeon run*

Frozen in each town and village in the central square,
Never in a dark museum but in the open air
A monument to mortal glories and wars that we have won.
Surely all of us have heard the stories of how his deeds were done
   Oh, pigeon run.

The day that they unveiled his statue and the bands that played
We all heard the widow weeping while the mayor prayed.
The words they chiseled in the marble were shadows in the sun, saying:
"Of all our boys who went to battle, here's the bravest one."
   Oh, pigeon run.

     Pigeons perch upon his shoulder
     The boy who's never growing older
     An old man comes to scrub the stains
     But when he's gone they're back again.

The boy who'd never be forgotten, the boy who knew no fear.
For charging when the bugle blew he gets a wreath each year.
And there he stands through all the seasons clutching at his gun,
Stone cold blind, but that's the reason he's on pigeon run
   Oh, pigeon run.

     Pigeons perch upon his shoulder
     They spread his head with fertilizer
     But no hair grows upon his head
     Nothing grows when you are dead.

48. *a better place to be*

It was an early morning barroom, the place had just opened up,
And a little man come in so fast and started at his cups.

The broad who served the whiskey was a big, old friendly girl,
Who tried to fight her empty nights by smiling at the world.

And she said, "Hey Bub, it's been awhile since you've been around.
Where the hell you been hiding, and why do you look so down?"

But the little man just sat there like he never heard a sound.

The waitress, she give out a cough, and acting not the least put off,
She spoke once again, "I don't want to bother you, consider it understood—
I know I'm not no beauty queen, but I sure can listen good."

The little man took his drink in his hand and raised it to his lips,
He took a couple of sips, and he told the waitress this story:

   I am the midnight watchman down at Miller's Tool and Die,
   I watch the metal rusting and I watch the time go by.
   A week ago at the diner, I stopped to get a bite,
   And this here lovely lady, she sat two seats from my right.
   And Lord, Lord, Lord, she was alright!

   She was so damn beautiful that she'd warm a winter frost,
   But she was long past lonely, and well nigh on to lost.
   Now I'm not much of a mover, or a pick-em-up-easy guy,
   But I decided to glide on over and give her one good try.
   And Lord, Lord, Lord, she was worth a try.

   Tongue-tied like a schoolboy, I stammered out some words,
   But it didn't really matter much, 'cause I don't think she heard.
   She just looked clear on through me to a space back in my head,
   It shamed me into silence, and quietly she said,
   "If you want me to come with you then that's alright with me,
   'Cause I know I'm going nowhere and anywhere's a better place to be.

I drove her to my boardinghouse, I took her up to my room,
I went to turn on the only light to brighten up the gloom,
But she said, "Please leave the light off, I don't mind the dark,"
And as her clothes all tumbled 'round her I could hear my heart.

The moonlight shone upon her as she lay back in my bed.
It was the kind of scene I only had imagined in my head.
I just could not believe it, to think that she was real.
And as I tried to tell her, she said, "Sshh, I know just how you feel.

And if you want to come here with me then that's alright with me,
'Cause I've been oh, so lonely, loving someone is a better way to be.

The morning came so swiftly and I held her in my arms.
She slept like a baby, snug and safe from harm.
I did not want to share her with the world or break the mood,
So before she woke I went out and bought us both some food.

I came back with my paper bag to find that she was gone.
She'd left a six-word letter saying, "It's time that I moved on."

The waitress took her bar rag and she wiped it across her eyes,
And as she spoke her voice came out as something like a sigh.

She said, "I wish that I was beautiful or that you were halfway blind,
I wish I weren't so doggone fat, I wish that you were mine.
And I wish that you'd come with me when I leave for home
Cause we both know all about emptiness and living all alone."

The little man looked at the empty glass in his hand,
And he smiled a crooked grin. He said, "I guess I'm out of gin,
And I know we both have been...so lonely.

And if you want me to come with you then that's alright with me,
Cause I know I'm going nowhere and anywhere's a better place to be."

49. *the baby never cries*

I've sung out one more evening
and I'm wrung out feeling beat.
I walk on out the door once more
to an empty city street.
A good guitar will serve you well
when you're living in the light
but it's never going to warm you
in the middle of the night.

So I come and go with her in whispers.
Each and every time she says she dies.
When she is reborn again I kiss her
and the baby never cries.

She works in the daytime,
she leaves her baby with a friend.
I sing every evening
I only see her now and then.
I come to her at midnight
when half the world's asleep
and she puts me back together
in the hours before I leave.

Her apartment is down on Perry Street
there is a tree in her back yard.
And it rubs the bedroom window
when the wind is blowing hard.
Her old man had left her,
he just took off for the coast
and I caught her on the rebound,
when I needed her the most.

50. *any old kind of day*

Turning on my pillow, thinking kind of strange
The color is of midnight in this room.
The cars outside are coughing and it's kind of hard to sleep.
There's neon out the window, not the moon.

It was just an any old kind of day.
The kind that comes and slips away.
The kind that fills up easy my life's time.
The night brought any old kind of dark.
I heard the ticking of my heart.
Then why am I thinking something's left behind?

I whistled round today, and skipped my footloose jig
To the hurdy-gurdy music of the street.
I looked up past the rooftops and saw my cloudless sky
But I keep on asking why
My life is passing by
And I'm left up high and dry
But it ain't no use to cry
So I shrug the same old sigh
And trust to things that other days will meet.

The night has had its laughing when streetlights blind the stars
So now it's shedding rain to sing its sorrow.
It's time for me to sleep and to rest these thoughts away
There'll be another day
When things will go my way
And there's other things to say
And other songs to play
And there'll be time enough for thinking come tomorrow.

51. *mr. tanner*

Mr. Tanner was a cleaner from a town in the midwest.
Of all the cleaning shops around, he'd made his the best.
He also was a baritone who sang while hanging clothes.
He practiced scales while pressing tails and sang at local shows.
His friends and neighbors praised the voice that poured out from his throat.
They said that he should use his gift instead of cleaning coats.

But music was his life It was not his livelihood,
And it made him feel so happy and it made him feel so good.
He sang from his heart and he sang from his soul.
He did not know how well he sang, it just made him whole.

His friends kept working on him to try music out full time.
A big debut and rave reviews, a great career to climb.
Finally they got to him, he would take the fling.
A concert agent in New York agreed to have him sing.
There were plane tickets, phone calls, money spent to rent the hall.
It took most of his savings, but he would have gladly used them all.

The evening came he took the stage, his face set in a smile.
In the half-filled hall the critics sat, watching on the aisle.
The concert was a blur to him, spatters of applause.
He did not know how well he sang, he only heard the flaws.
But the critics were concise it only took four lines.
And no one could accuse them of being over kind.

"Mr. Martin Tanner, baritone, of Dayton Ohio
made his town hall debut last night.
He came well prepared but unfortunately his presentation
was not up to contemporary professional standards.
His voice lacks the range of tonal color to make it consistently interesting.
Full time consideration of another endeavor might be in order."

He came home to Dayton and was questioned by his friends.
But he smiled and just said nothing and he never sang again.
Excepting very late at night when the shop was dark and closed.
He sang softly to himself as he sorted through the clothes.

52. *mail order annie*

At first I did not think it could be you.
But you're the only one that got off the train.
So you must be my wife Miss Annie Halsey
Yes, I guess I am your husband. Hello I'm Harry Crane.

Mail Order Annie, never mind your crying.
Your tears are sweet rain in my empty life.
Mail Order Annie, can't you see I'm trying
To tell you that I'm glad you're here,
You who are the woman who's come to be my wife.

You are the woman who's come to be my wife.

You know you're not as pretty as I dreamed you'd be,
But then I'm not no handsome fancy Dan.
And out here looks are really not important.
It's what's inside a woman when she's up against the land.

You know it's not no easy life you're entering.
The winter wind comes whistling through the cracks
            there in the sod.
You know you'll never have too many neighbors.
There's you Girl, and there's me,
            and there's God.

I know I'm just a dirt man from the North Dakota plains.
You're one girl from the city who's been thrown out
            on her own.
I'm standing here not sure of what to say to you
'Cepting Mail Order Annie, let's you and me go home.

53. *what made america famous*

It was the town that made America famous.
The churches full and the kids all going to hell.
Six traffic lights and seven cops and all the streets kept clean.
The supermarket and the drug store and the bars all doing well.
   They were the folks that made America famous.
   The local fire department stocked with shorthaired volunteers.
   And on Saturday night while America boozes
   The fire department showed dirty movies,
   The lawyer and the grocer seeing their dreams
   Come to life on the movie screens
   While the plumber hopes that he won't be seen
   As he tries to hide his fears and he wipes away his tears.
      But something's burning somewhere. Does anybody care?

We were the kids that made America famous.
The kind of kids that long since drove our parents to despair.
We were lazy long hairs dropping out, lost confused and copping out
Convinced our futures were in doubt and trying not to care.
   We lived in the house that made America famous.
   It was a rundown slum, the shame of all the decent folks in town.
   We hippies and some welfare cases,
   Crowded families of coal black faces,
   Cramped inside some cracked old boards,
   The best that we all could afford
   But still too fine for the rich landlord
   To ever tear it down and we could hear the sound
      Of something burning somewhere. Is anybody there?

We all lived the life that made America famous.
Our cops would make a point to shadow us around our town.
And we love children put a swastika on the bright red firehouse door.
America the beautiful, it make a body proud.

And then came the night that made America famous.
Was it carelessness or just someone's sick idea of a joke.
In the tinder box trap that we hippies lived in someone struck a spark.
At first I thought that I was dreaming,
Then I saw the first flames gleaming
And heard the sound of children screaming
Coming through the smoke. That's when the horror broke.
    Something's burning somewhere. Does anybody care?
It was the fire that made America famous.
The sirens wailed and the firemen stumbled sleepy from their homes.
And the plumber yelled: "Come on let's go!"
But they saw what was burning and said: "Take it slow,
Let 'em sweat a little, they'll never know
And besides, we just cleaned the chrome." Said the plumber: "I'm going alone."

He rolled on up in the fire truck
And raised the ladder to the ledge
Where me and my girl and a couple of kids
Were clinging like bats to the edge.
We staggered to salvation,
Collapsed on the street.
And I never thought that a fat man's face
would ever look so sweet.

It was the scene that made America famous.
If not the love that made America great.

You see we spent that night in the home of a man I'd never known before.
It's funny when you get that close it's kind of hard to hate.
   I went to sleep with the hope that made America famous.
   I had the kind of a dream that maybe they're still trying to teach
       in school.
   Of the America that made America famous...and
   Of the people who just might understand
   That how together yes we can
   Create a country better than
   The one we have made of this land,
   We have the choice to make each man
   who dares to dream, reaching out his hand
   A prophet or just a crazy God damn
   Dreamer of a fool—yes a crazy fool.

        There's something burning somewhere.
        Does anybody care?
        Is anybody there?

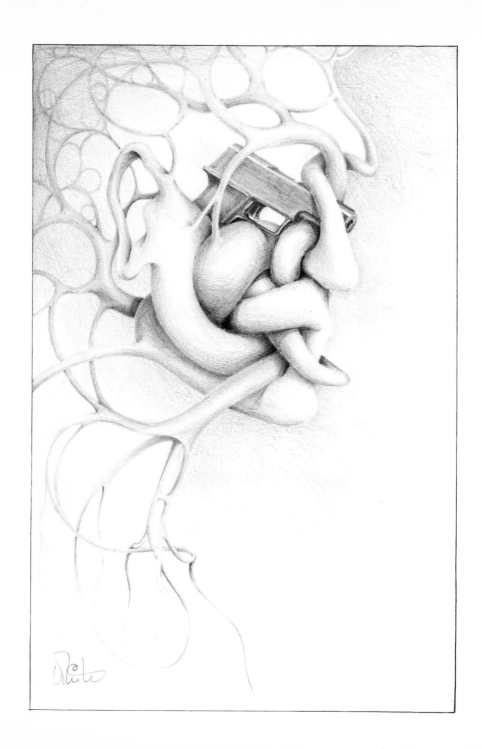

54. *sniper*

It is an early Monday morning,
The sun is becoming bright on the land.
No one is watching as he comes walking,
Two bulky suitcases hang from his hands.
He heads toward the tower that stands in the campus,
Goes through the door and starts up the stairs.
The sound of his footsteps, the sound of his breathing,
The sound of the silence, for no one was there.

    I didn't really know him, he was kinda strange,
    Always sort of sat there, he never seemed to change.

He reached the catwalk, he put down his burden.
The four-sided clock began to chime.
Seven a.m., the day is beginning,
So much to do, and so little time.
He looks at the city where no one had known him,
He looks at the sky where no one looks down.
He looks at his life and what it had shown him,
He looks for his shadow; it cannot be found.

    He was such a moody child, very hard to touch,
    Even as a baby he never smiled too much. No, no.

      "You bug me," she said. "You're ugly," she said.
      "Please hug me," I said, but she just sat there,
      With the same flat stare, that she saves for me alone,
      When I'm home.

He laid out the rifles, he loaded his shotgun,
He stacked up the cartridges along the wall.
He knew he would need them for his conversation.
If it went as he planned then he might use them all.
He said:

      "Listen you people, I've got a question.
      You won't pay attention, but I'll ask anyhow.
      I've got a way that will get me an answer.
      I've been waiting to ask you 'til now. Right now!
      Am I? I am a lover who's never been kissed.
      Am I? I am a fighter who's not made a fist.
      Am I? If I'm alive then there's so much I've missed.
      How do I know I exist?
      Are you listening to me? are you listening to me?
      Am I?

The first words he spoke took the town by surprise.
One got Mrs. Gibbons above her right eye.
It blew her through the window, wedged her against the door,
Reality pouring from her face, staining the floor.

    He was kinda creepy, sort of a dunce,
    Met him at a corner bar, I only dated the poor boy once,
    Just once. That was all.

Bill Wedon was questioned as he stepped from his car.
Tom Scott ran across the street, but he never got that far.
The police were there in minutes, they set up barricades.
But he spoke right on over them, in a half mile circle,
In that dumbstruck city, his pointed questions were sprayed.

He knocked over Danny Tyson, as he ran toward the noise,
And just about then the answers started coming, sweet, sweet, joy!
Thudding in the clock face, whining off the walls.
Reaching up to where he sat, their answering calls.
Thirty-seven people got his message so far.
Yes, he was reaching them, right where they are.

They set up an assault team; they asked for volunteers,
They had to go and get him, that much was clear.
And the word spread about him on radio and TV.
In appropriately sober tones they asked, "WHO CAN HE BE?"

    He was a very dull boy, very taciturn.
    Not much of a joiner. He did not want to learn. No, no.

        "They're coming to get me, they don't want to let me,
        Stay in the bright light too long.
        It's getting on noon now, it's going to be soon now.
        But oh, what a wonderful song.

        Mama, won't you nurse me,
        Rain me down the sweet milk of your kindness.
        Mama, it's getting worse for me,
        Won't you please make me warm and mindless.
        Mama, yes, you have cursed me.
        I never will forgive you for your blindness.
        I HATE YOU!

The wires are all humming for me,
And I can hear them coming for me,
Soon they'll be here, but there's nothing to fear.
No, not anymore, though they've blasted the door!"

s the copter dropped the gas, he shouted, "Who cares!"
hey could hear him laughing as they started up the stairs.
hey stormed out of the doorway, blinking at the sun.
'ith one final fusillade, their answer had come....

"Am I—there is no way that you can hide me.
Am I—though you have put your fire inside me,
You've given me my answer, can't you see.
I was, I am. And now, I WILL BE!"

autobiographical notes

Harry Chapin: I've been a looker, if not a seer, for most of
my thirty-three years. In the process, I have attempted in
writing and other forms to capture many different people and
experiences, and discovered that my virtues as a creator lay
not in genius but in blind perseverance. I hope the reader will
find I have persevered enough in the creation of these poems.

Rob White: At one time I was a landscape architect
struggling with the straight lines and practicality of design
inherent in that profession. This book is the first occasion I've
had to wallow in the impractical. I'm grateful to Harry for the
opportunity.